PRIVATE EYE

Colemanballs

7

A selection of quotes,
most of which originally appeared
in PRIVATE EYE's
'Colemanballs' column.

Our thanks once again to all
the readers who sent us their
contributions.

COLEMANBALLS TOP TEN

PLACE	NAME	ENTRIES
1	DAVID COLEMAN	98
2	MURRAY WALKER	62
3	SIMON BATES	51
4	TED LOWE	37
5	RON PICKERING	27
6	PETER JONES	23
7	HARRY CARPENTER	22
8	BRIAN MOORE	21
9	BRYON BUTLER	15
10	TREVOR BAILEY	14
11	FRANK BRUNO	12
12	ELTON WELSBY	9

COMPOSITE TOTAL FIGURES COMPILED BY THE NEASDEN INSTITUTE OF STATISTICS, E&OE

PRIVATE EYE

Colemanballs 7

Compiled and edited by
BARRY FANTONI

Illustrated by Larry

PRIVATE EYE • CORGI

Published in Great Britain
by Private Eye Productions Ltd,
6 Carlisle Street, London W1V 5RG,
in association with Corgi Books

©1994 Pressdram Ltd
ISBN 0 552 14279 4
Designed by Bridget Tisdall
Printed in Great Britain by
Cox and Wyman Ltd, Reading

Corgi Books are published by Transworld Publishers Ltd,
61-63 Uxbridge Road, Ealing, London W5 5SA,
in Australia by Transworld Publishers (Australia) Pty, Ltd,
15-23 Helles Avenue, Moorebank, NSW 2170
and in New Zealand by Transworld Publishers (N.Z.) Ltd,
Cnr. Moselle and Waipareira Avenues, Henderson, Auckland

2 4 6 8 10 9 7 5 3 1

Athletics

"Carl Lewis, what a good runner... All his arms and elbows and knees running in the same direction."

COMMENTATOR

"Michael Jordan, one of the world's greatest defenders — if not one of the best..."

DAVID COLEMAN

"John Regis has smashed Linford's UK record — he's equalled it."

DAVID COLEMAN

"Our athletes are flying the flagship for British sport."

FATIMA WHITBREAD

"...Maycock may have been making the wrong mistakes tactically in the past."

STEVE OVETT

"The pacemaker shook everyone by staying in front and finishing third."

DAVID COLEMAN

"So, it's five 1,000 metre laps, plus a bit to make up the 5,000 metres."

R. COLEMAN

"Linford Christie must be thinking, at 32, can he emulate what Ottey just failed to do."

JOHN WALKER

"Linford Christie, the fastest man in the world in 1992. Other men may have run faster this year."

DAVID COLEMAN

"At the English Schools Athletic Championships, you can see the youngsters of the future."

DAVID COLEMAN

"I was keeping my legs and fingers crossed for him."

DAVID COLEMAN

"It's a race that the Kenyans have dominated — but, looking at the records, it's the first time they've won it."

DAVID COLEMAN

Boxing

"Boxing's all about getting the job done as quickly as possible — whether it takes 10 or 15 or 20 rounds."

FRANK BRUNO

"It'll go the distance, and Lewis will win on a late stoppage."

FRANK BRUNO

"He is taking me so serious, he is fighting under closed doors."

LENNOX LEWIS

"So, is Frank [Bruno] a contender with a capital 'c', a small 'c' or no 'c' at all?"

JOHN INVERDALE

"I know I've got the power and technology to beat him [Lennox Lewis]."

FRANK BRUNO

"He [Frank Bruno] has a lot of fans out there, and I have a lot of fans out there, and they both want to see it go ahead."

LENNOX LEWIS

"The game's not over till the fat lady plays the piano. Tonight Chris Eubank played the piano."
BARRY HEARN

"Michael Armstrong is a keen supporter of boxing, unlike his ring namesake Chris Eubank."
REG GUTTERIDGE

"The power worries me, but I don't go in there worrying about the power or anything."
LENNOX LEWIS

Cricket

"Chris Lewis didn't bowl, then came in and scored thirty. A top all-round effort."

ALEC STEWART

"I thought he was going to dive and decapitate himself... badly."

MIKE HENDRICK

"If England lose now they'll be leaving the field with their heads between their legs."

GEOFF BOYCOTT, SKY TV

"Ah yes, sledging... In the days before the microphones on the pitch, we got that blind MP chap up into the commentary box to lip-read..."

BRIAN JOHNSTON

"Jon Lewis, a real Essex boy there... born in Isleworth, Middlesex."

TONY LEWIS

"Now this next question has absolutely nothing to do with either music or sport... at what ground did Geoffrey Boycott hit his hundredth 100?"

CLASSIC FM

"Australia must now climb to the top diving board for a last desperate throw of the dice."

BOB WILLIS

"Hick and Atherton are a good pair of hands."

CRICKET COMMENTATOR

"He's a very dangerous bowler — innocuous, if you like."

DAVID LLOYD

"I don't think I've ever seen anything quite like that before — it's the second time it's happened today."

BRIAN JOHNSTON

"The batting side find it easier to bat in bad light than the fielding side do."

TREVOR BAILEY

"Such an easy pitch... Graham Gooch and Alec Stewart think their Christmases have all come home."

GEOFF BOYCOTT

"My cricket's all been played in a triangle of about two or three square miles."

PHIL CARRICK

"Defreitas... just in the back of his mind he is wearing a support."

GEOFF BOYCOTT

"Here he comes — racing in like an express train down the runway..."

CRICKET COMMENTATOR

Cycling

"Ten [Tour de France] riders crashed, two retired after falls, another dropped out when diarrhoea slowed him to the point of elimination..."

JAMES RICHARDSON

"He's coming on in fits and bounds."

PHIL LIGGETT

Darts

"They can land darts on the nucleus of a proton."

COMMENTATOR, BBC2

DOUGIE DONNELLY: John Lowe, you're now three times world darts champion. What does that mean to you?
JOHN LOWE: It means I'm three times world darts champion!

BBC

Electionballs

"I was polled on the amount of radio I watched..."
EMMA FREUD

"We're not the sort of party that does deals behind smoke-filled doors."
BRIAN GOULD

"The conservatives fear they maybe-side tracked by a storm in a egg-cup."

JOHN COLE

"The British public sees with blinding clarity."
MICHAEL HESELTINE

"We said zero, and I think any statistician will tell you that, when you're dealing with very big numbers, zero must mean plus or minus a few."
WILLIAM WALDEGRAVE

"Let me explain, Nick — it is the key which turns the door in the lock."

PADDY ASHDOWN

Q: Which of these words do you think best sums up your character?
PADDY ASHDOWN: Er... perhaps 'decisive'?

CHANNEL 4

"...and now the declaration from Berwick-upon-Tweed, Britain's most northerly constituency."

DAVID DIMBLEBY

Football

"He [Chelsea goalkeeper] does not speak too much English but, once he gets hold of the language, he will be the best goalkeeper in the country."

RADIO 4

"Whether that was a penalty or not, the referee thought otherwise."

BRIAN MOORE

"Bruce, on his right foot, is still running..."

ALAN GREEN

"Des Walker knows that Signori has all the tricks up his book."

RAY WILKINS

"You're either very good or very bad. There's no in between. We were in between."

GARY LINEKER

"Mancini seems to have ten yards under his shorts."

RAY WILKINS

"34-year-old Alan Cork steps up to take the
penalty. Thin on top but thick in mind and body."
                                        COMMENTATOR

"If in winning the game we only finish with a draw
we would be fine."
                                        JACK CHARLTON

"He [Alan Shearer] could be at 100% fitness, but
not peak fitness."
                                        GRAHAM TAYLOR

"He really had to wrap his head around that cross."
                                        COMMENTATOR

"If only he'd chanced his arm with his left leg."
                                    TREVOR BROOKING

"Because of the booking, I will miss the Holland game — if selected."
                                    PAUL GASCOIGNE

"The half-time whistles are pealing all over the country."
                                    ELTON WELSBY

"And Hately rose like Buddha at the far post to power that header just over the bar."

ALAN HANSEN

"The game kicks off when it kicks off and when it kicks off it's over."

TOM TYRALL

"There's a little bit of nitty gritty flying about, which is nice to see."

RAY WILKINS

"My name is the one people normally have at the end of their lips."

IAN WRIGHT

"He [Ron Atkinson] describes him [Sean Teale] as John Wayne — the man who comes over the hill to save the cavalry."

ALAN PARRY

ANDY SMITH: So at the end of the day, why do you think Arsenal won?
GEORGE GRAHAM: Because we scored 2 goals and Sheffield Wednesday scored 1.

RADIO 4

"He [Peter Swales] has now got a scapegoat to hang his hat on."

FRANCIS LEE

"We were all unanimous — well, you two were."
ELTON WELSBY

"...the Moroccan-born Nayim scored his second goal... and the Spanish-born Nayim made it a hat-trick as he scored his third goal."
BILL MCFARLAND

"All that remains is for a few dots and commas to be crossed and I'll be back at the club where my career began."
MITCHELL THOMAS

"He was chased nearly ten yards through the six-yard box."
ANDY GRAY

"Obviously... supporters running on the pitch... leaves a sour taste in everybody's mind."
ALAN SMITH

"Winning doesn't really matter as long as you win."
VINNY JONES

"They [Millwall] never fail to disappoint me."
DAVID PLEAT

"Whatever the result tonight I think Reading will be the winners."
COMMENTATOR

"The supporters will be in great expectation of what they expect..."
BOBBY GOULD

"It was one of those goals that's invariably a goal."
DENIS LAW

"Ian [Snodin] and I have both been out injured.
He's put on weight and I've lost it and vice versa."
RONNIE WHELAN

"And that's Cantona's fourth consecutive goal in
the Premier League."
JOHN MOTSON

"He always has a look on his face of some sort..."
FOOTBALL COMMENTATOR

"It's a case of putting all our eggs into the next ninety minutes."

PHIL NEAL

ELTON WELSBY: Magnifique, Eric.
ERIC CANTONA: Oh, do you speak French?
ELTON WELSBY: Non.

ITV

"It was a terrible challenge. He had his legs decapitated."

COLIN GIBSON

"Leeds have got to shake off all the emotion they've been drained of over the last few days."

TONY GUBBA

"As I say, if we score more goals than them then we'll win."

KENNY DALGLISH

"We always consider a point dropped at home as a point dropped."

WALTER SMITH

"A brain scan has revealed Andrew Caddick is not suffering from a stress fracture of the shin."

JO SHELDON

"Maybe just one goal would be enough to break the deadlock..."

ALAN PARRY

"Ian Snodin, who played as one of a three-man back four in the first half..."

RON JONES

"It's a very flat three-man back four."

GORDON COX

JIM ROSENTHAL: So what's an American doing
playing in goal for Millwall?
AMERICAN GOALIE: I'm trying to keep the ball
out.

ITV

"It's a shame half-time came as early as it did."
GORDON DURY

"He came on a free transfer and has been giving
good value for money."
CLIVE ALLEN

"And that's Aston Villa's first League goal since their last one."

ELTON WELSBY

"He'd no alternative but to make a needless tackle..."

PAUL ELIOT

"It wouldn't be a surprise to see Marseilles play a rough game, but it would be surprising if they did."

CHRIS WADDLE

"We showed what English footballers and English football is all about. We played the Continentals at their own game."

GEORGE GRAHAM

"The drought which has plagued Manchester United all season now seems to have evaporated."

JAMES REEVES

"Venison and Butcher — they're both as brave as two peas in a pod."

JOHN SILLETT

RON ATKINSON: It's a difficult time for George Graham. Does he gamble and... for me, I would definitely bring Limpars on.
BRIAN MOORE: Well, Ron, what would you do?
RON ATKINSON: I'd bring Limpars on.

ITV

"Pallister's an excellent centre half, particularly upstairs."

RON ATKINSON

"I'd say he is the best in Europe, if you put me on the fence."

BOBBY ROBSON

"His return gives England another key to its bow."

STUART PEARCE

"Sunderland are suffering from déjà vu — a case of 'What will be, will be'."

LENNIE LAWRENCE

"A late consolation goal for Middlesbrough — they won't take any consolation from that."

RAY STUBBS

Golf

"Nick Faldo has shown himself to be a worthy world No.1 by finishing second here today."

COMMENTATOR

"The Great White Shark could be a dark horse."

IAN BAKER FINCH

"These golfers don't mind a little rain as long as it's not raining at the same time."

BRUCE CRITCHELY

"Although it's a narrow green, it's a wide green."

PETER ALLIS

Horse Racing

"As they say, Derby Day comes but once a year, and that's true in every sense."

CHANNEL 4 COMMENTATOR

Literally

"…and I went back to the Isle of Man quite
literally with my tail between my legs."

J.P. DONLEAVY

"Wimbledon, caught with their knickers down in the first minute, literally."

BOBBY MOORE

"Last time out he won at Folkestone, literally pulling a bus..."

LORD OAKSEY

"William Byrd, who literally had the ear of Elizabeth the First..."

PRESENTER, CLASSIC-FM

"Everyone has their ears glued to their radios —
quite literally."

STEPHEN SACKER

"Blackburn Rovers are now taking Brian Clough's
team literally to the cleaners."

BRIAN CLARKE

"They've got million-year-old eggs here [in Hong
Kong]. And that's literally what they are."

SIMON BATES

"Literally, Sir George, a yes or no answer — is this
a long-term or a short-term measure?"

VALERIE SINGLETON

"Here under the roof at Earls Court is quite
literally the whole world of boating."

MIKE SMITH

"I'll leave the atmosphere to your imagination, but
you can literally touch it."

ELTON WELSBY

"The orchestra has left the platform, literally as one man."

CHRIS DE SOUSA

Motor Sport

"Mansell is now on his 62nd lap. After this: laps 63, 64 and 65."

MURRAY WALKER

"On a scale of one to ten, it's more confusing over here than in Europe."

NIGEL MANSELL

"He [Damon Hill] is leading and behind him are the second and third men."

MURRAY WALKER

"Either the car is stationary or it's on the move."

MURRAY WALKER

"Historically, this track is two seconds quicker tomorrow."

NIGEL MANSELL

MURRAY WALKER: When did you first become aware you had a puncture?
DAMON HILL: When the tyre went down, Murray.

BBC2

"In the first Grand Prix in the 30s at Donnington there was an unprecedented crowd."

MURRAY WALKER

"Once again Damon Hill is modest in defeat."
                                    MURRAY WALKER

"The status quo could well be as it was before..."
                                    MURRAY WALKER

Oddballs

"There's nothing like seeing two protagonists
having a nose to nose tête à tête."
                                    RICHARD SKINNER

"The National Museum of Photography, Film and
Television is tremendously important, both in
photography, television and film."
                        SIR RICHARD ATTENBOROUGH

"You sometimes open your mouth and it punches
you straight between the eyes…"
                                    PADDY CRERAND

"The BBC is marching on all four cylinders."

JOHN BIRT

"I've been bitten by the ferocious tongue of Frank Rich."

MICHAEL PRAED

"You can't beat the tidal wave when the avalanche comes down the mountain."

ROBERT KILROY-SILK

"It certainly has proved a bed of nails, and Sir James feels that it is time for a clean sheet."
DAVID DAVIES

"Let's see if we can find someone who speaks braille..."
ANNEKA RICE

"What's the plural of 'ignited'?"
GABY ROSLIN

"Anybody in their right mind who doesn't ask you needs his head examined."
SEAN RAFFERTY

"Now? With McGarrett breathing down my neck like a ton of bricks!"

HAWAII 5-0

"The window of opportunity will be blown completely out of the water."

GERALDINE KENNEDY

"Has suicide become a way of life in British prisons?"

PETER GLANVILLE

"And this is the real carrot at the end of the rainbow."

PAUL LYNEHAM

"It's a part of Spain that's forever England — the car park's full of Volvos."

CLIVE TULLOH

"I'm here 13 days and I haven't been to the same restaurant once."

TERRY WOGAN

"Make or break situations — such as we have seen here — can sometimes make as well as break."

ROBIN OAKLEY

"Oh, come on now — he's talking about blacks. Let's call a spade a spade."

GERALD HARPER

"It [Have I Got News For You] has a huge audience, which means quite a lot of people watch it."

IAN HISLOP

"I shall fight every tooth and nail I find."
SHOP STEWARD, LEYLAND-DAF

"Well, he wasn't an obvious homosexual. I mean, he didn't push it down people's... er... noses."
EX-WIFE OF JIMMY EDWARDS

"I was insufficiently insensitive to the concerns of staff."
JOHN BIRT

"There's nothing wrong with pregnancy. Half the people wouldn't be here today if it wasn't for women being pregnant."

SARAH KENNEDY

"The sands of time are chiming towards the twenty-first century."

SALLY JESSY RAPHAEL

"We've been sold down the garden path."

NIGEL KENNEDY

"But speaking of tomorrow, let's hark back to yesterday."

DANNY BAKER

"So you went to the hospital about your alcoholism problem. That must have taken a lot of bottle!"

JUDY FINNEGAN

"Last night was her debut at Covent Garden and, my goodness, it won't be her last."

HENRY KELLY

"It's not only a race against the clock, but a race against time itself."

PRESENTER, BBC WALES

"The next rise in mortgage rates will probably be an increase."

REPRESENTATIVE, CBI

"Salman Rushdie knew exactly what he was doing... he was playing with fire, sailing close to the wind and sticking his neck out."

TOBY JESSEL

"A tabloid newspaper can usually expect to go down with all hands blazing."

RICHARD STOTT

"A winning formula is not something you can write an equation for."

MAGGIE BROWN

"We appeal for anyone who may or may not have seen anything suspicious to come forward."

POLICE OFFICER, RADIO 4

"You mention these talks as a carrot. Surely the carrot has now been extinguished?"

INTERVIEWER

"...no one to stem the floodgates of hot air; there is now an avalanche of it."

CAROL THATCHER

"I looked at it and saw, at once, that it was a can of worms in a nutshell."

PAUL BOWER

"You can sum up today's weather in just two words... dry, bright and sunny in most areas with a chance of light showers in the north.

FRANCES WILSON

"He [Francis Bacon] was probably our greatest living painter — until he died."

NEWS READER, LBC

"The car is the only means of transport for the rural motorist."

SPOKESMAN, ROAD HAULAGE INDUSTRY

"Profitable businesses are going bankrupt all over the country."

RICHARD LITTLEJOHN

"He's at an age now when most people just want to put their feet in an armchair."

JIM MCGRATH

"I'm hopeless at telling the time — I need a digital clock with capital letters."

RICHARD LITTLEJOHN

"One bad apple can tar the rest of us."
COMMENTATOR, RADIO SCOTLAND

"I think you've hit the nose on the nail there.
KEVIN GREENING, GLR

"Shelley's grave is in Christchurch, so there's life in Christchurch..."
DAVID DIMBLEBY

"Britain's premier earl, the Duke of Norfolk."
DEREK JAMESON

"...even though it's only acting, it's full of drama."
CARON KEATING

"Here...[in London]... we're not dealing in dollars, we're dealing in pounds, shillings and pence."
RICHARD LITTLEJOHN

"Stravinsky grabs our ears by the throat."
ROGER NICHOLS, RADIO 3

"...when someone comes up behind you with a knife and threatens you at gunpoint."
PETER MANDELSON

"The church of the Nativity naturally post-dates the birth of Jesus."
COMMENTATOR, THE TRAVEL SHOW

"And what shape, then, is the Rubik's Cube?"
PETER SISSONS

"Today we look at virginity, and losing it for the first time."

RICHARD MADELEY

"It's a drip, drip, drip chipping away at the BBC."
HAMISH MCCRAE

"I got up more nostrils than there are noses."
ANDREW NEILL

"This huge row of atomic proportions…"
DAVID FROST

Olympicballs

"...and Tulu... looking a lot more experienced, although she's not showing it tonight."

DAVID COLEMAN

"The Spaniard wins in 3 minutes 40.12... the slowest possible winning time you can imagine."

DAVID COLEMAN

"It's a great advantage to be able to hurdle with both legs."

DAVID COLEMAN

"I don't think he's ever lost a race at 200 metres,
except at 400..."

DAVID COLEMAN

"Well, Burkart in the red — not only did he play it
safely, he played it dangerously."

DAVID COLEMAN

"Burrell is clinically blind in his right eye...
Christie is on his left side. He'll have Christie in
full vision."

DAVID COLEMAN

"There's a mistake on the scoreboard: they're only
showing his Christian names, Ismail Ibrahim."

DAVID COLEMAN

"He's been out for two years and as the Olympic athlete said, 'That's not just two years but two times three hundred and sixty-five days'."

IAN DARKE

"And there is Linford Christie on the warm up track outside — well, in his case he'll be warming down because the final does not start for around 75 minutes."

DAVID COLEMAN

"For the last two seasons she has been running on painkillers — her foot is quite sore."

DAVID COLEMAN

"...and if Berger gets another yellow flag it will be a red one."

DAVID COLEMAN

"It must be harder to hurdle something that isn't there than something that is there."

DAVID MOORCROFT

"There he is, the fastest man in the world this year... other men may have run faster this year but he did it when it mattered."

DAVID COLEMAN

"After the initial rush for places, they're settling down now to sensibility."

DAVID COLEMAN

"He has just moved up the field from 25th to 30th."

DAVID COLEMAN

"Indeed, they've put a blanket round the entire city."

DAVID COLEMAN

Politics

"We have got to all work together in the national interest and get away from the everyday bump and grind of politics."

PADDY ASHDOWN

GLR REPORTER: What should you do if your children want to talk about solvent abuse?
HEALTH MINISTER BRIAN MAWHINNEY: Take a deep breath...

GLR NEWS

"It's almost like a guillotine... the trap door opens and you're gone."

KEN LIVINGSTONE

"They [the IRA] are deadly serious about a cessation of violence."

JOHN HUME

"It's important to allay the finger of responsibility at the door of parents."

JOHN PATTEN

"How mortally wounded is John Major..."
JEREMY PAXMAN

"We live in a world where the Kelloggs Cornflake family is ever less rare."
VIRGINIA BOTTOMLEY

"British unemployment is rising faster here than in any other European country!"
NEIL KINNOCK

"That part of it is behind us now... I'm drawing a line under the sand."
JOHN MAJOR

"The trend in the rise in unemployment is downward."

GILLIAN SHEPHERD

"The condition of the country wasn't handed down in tablets of stone from Mount Olympus."

MARGARET BECKETT

"Will Mr Major be flying back from Bonn with the scent of victory in his sails?"

JON SNOW

"The German Chancellor, Helmut Kohl, was pelted with eggs when he attended a rally in Berlin today. He was whisked away by police."

NEWSREADER, CLASSIC FM

"There is always a choice of whether one does it last week, this week, or next week."

JOHN MAJOR

"They put a knife into a Minister again and again and again until he's hanged."

JILL KNIGHT

"We are not wholly an island, except geographically."

JOHN MAJOR

"The Thatcher household did not spend 24 hours a day discussing politics over the early morning tea."

CAROL THATCHER

"Bringing up children on your own is very difficult, even when there are two parents."

VIRGINIA BOTTOMLEY

"Party Conferences are the chance for the grass-roots to get their hobby-horses off their chest."

LIBERAL SPOKESMAN

"These cornerstones were the centre of the Chancellor's policy."

GORDON BROWN

"Suicide is a real threat to health in a modern society."

VIRGINIA BOTTOMLEY

"Open up that there Pandora's Box and there's no telling what Trojan Horses might come out of it."
PETER BROOKE

"Nobody who has seen the pictures can be remotely other than greatly concerned."
DOUGLAS HURD

"...This is a view that has been expressed by some very thoughtful people — as well as those in the House of Commons."
JOHN COLE

"It's not something you can do like a fairy godmother from the top of a Christmas tree."
MICHAEL HESELTINE

"They (the BBC) must blow their own trumpet and have others blow their own trumpet for them."
PAUL BOATENG

"This is Major's last desperate throw of the dice and we will ensure it scores a double blank."
JACK STRAW

"As I've said before and I said yesterday, this is one of the key questions which will be decided or not decided at Edinburgh."

DOUGLAS HURD

MIKE CARLTON: The question is which Cabinet Minister was pelted with eggs and orange juice at the London School of Economics last night? I'll give you a clue his first name is Peter."
CALLER: Is it Virginia Bottomley?

LBC

"But aren't these latest Maastricht moves a case of nailing the stable doors and hanging them up long after the horse has bolted?"

ANNOUNCER, RTE

"I with myself saw what the soldiers in Bosnia were doing."

MALCOLM RIFKIND

"I'm for a stronger death penalty."

PRESIDENT BUSH

"Teenage orphans are to be given a say in their future. Health Secretary Virginia Bottomley has announced new legislation that will allow them to stay in touch with their natural parents."

SKY NEWS

"I can definitely say, that had the police not been there this morning, there would have been no arrests."

ARTHUR SCARGILL

"All those people who say that there will never be a single European currency are trying to forecast history."

KENNETH CLARK

"It's one of the great urban myths that people get pregnant in order to have children."

MENZIES CAMPBELL QC

Pop

PAULA YATES: Your new single, "Let's Get Married"; what's it about?
THE PROCLAIMERS: Erm, getting married...

THE BIG BREAKFAST

"Well, listen, I heard something that I read the other day…"

TERRY CHRISTIAN

"A part of Jim Morrison refused to believe he was dead."

ROCK EXPERT, RADIO 5

"When you improvise, do you actually have to make it up?"

PAULA YATES

"I went to see it [Sunset Boulevard] with an open mind, thinking I wouldn't enjoy it."

PETE MURRAY

"So, can you point to anywhere on the map that's undiscovered?"

NICKY CAMPBELL

DJ: What type of gun was a Gatling Gun?
CONTESTANT: A sword.

LBC

"If you say 'charity work' nowadays it sounds such a double negative."

SIMON BATES

DAVID HEPWORTH: You were born in Europe, weren't you?
JACKSON BROWNE: That's right — Germany.
DAVID HEPWORTH: How come?
JACKSDON BROWNE: My parents were there at the time.

GLR

JUDY FINNIGAN: You say you've been in the Beach Boys for the past 32 years. How long is that exactly?
MIKE LOVE: Thirty-two years, I guess...
JUDY FINNIGAN: Really?

ITV

"Easter Day fell on a Sunday in 1987."

SIMON BATES

"Today is Reg Kray's birthday. Happy birthday, Reg. Not sure when his twin brother Ronnie's is, but best wishes to Ron anyway."

NICKY CAMPBELL

"The lights went up and there I was standing flat on my face."

JASON DONOVAN

GARY DAVIS: What have you done this weekend?
CALLER: I went out for a meal last night with Suzanne, my girlfriend.
GARY DAVIS: So is Suzanne your girlfriend?

VIRGIN 1215

"And now something to really get you in the mood for Barcelona — José Feliciano singing California Dreaming."

STEVE WRIGHT

"I've studied his lyrics note by note…"

GARY BARLOW

"Jim Reeves died on 31st July 1964, but his career was not affected by his death."

ED STEWART

"And tonight, Coltrane in a Cadillac, which is basically Robbie Coltrane in an open-top Buick."

SIMON BATES

JONATHAN KING: My new series goes out on Tuesday nights here on Radio One and it's called 'Music Music Music'.
SIMON BATES: What's it about?

RADIO 1

"Well, someone once said that all the world's a stage, and on the top 40 scene stage Michael Jackson drops one place."

DJ, CAPITAL RADIO

"It's coming back to you like a kangaroo."
NICKY CAMPBELL

DAVE LEE TRAVIS: Who played the title role in Educating Rita?
CONTESTANT: Is that a man or a woman, Dave?

RADIO 1

SIMON MAYO: Congratulations! You've just won 20 CD vouchers — what are you going to do with them?
CONTESTANT: Buy lots of CDs.

RADIO 1

"Hmm... I wonder what infinite density is? I suppose it's density that's infinite really."

SIMON BATES

"Apparently, they're totally functional: they don't actually do anything."

SIMON MAYO

BRIAN HAYES: If I were to blindfold you and play you one extract from a real Beatles song and one from a bootleg version, would you be able to tell the difference?
INTERVIEWEE: Why would I need a blindfold?

RADIO 4

JOHNNY WALKER: Do you think that if he [Buddy Holly] had lived he would still be as good now as he was then?
INTERVIEWEE: Yes, because although his career was going through a difficult stage, I'm sure that he wasn't about to crash and burn.

RADIO

"I'm only saying this once, so listen carefully. Then I'll repeat it."

SIMON BATES

KENNY EVERETT: Can you give me a place name that contains the letters A, G and I?
CALLER: Yugoslavia.
KENNY EVERETT: No, Yugoslavia doesn't have an 'A' in it.

CAPITAL GOLD

"The entire KLF catalogue has been deleted — suddenly and with ample warning."

STEVE WRIGHT

Question & Answer

CALLER: We actually have a 46-year-old world champion.
SIMON FANSHAWE: And how old is he?
CALLER: He's 46.

RADIO 5

INTERVIEWER: The top school in Britain is in the Scilly Isles. What does that tell us?
SPOKESMAN: The top school in Britain is in the Scilly Isles.

RADIO 1

CALLER: I have the autograph of Horatio Nelson.
EXPERT: And what does it say exactly?
CALLER: It says 'Horatio Nelson'.

LBC

JEREMY ISAACS: You called your autobiography 'The Ragman's Son'. Who was the Ragman?
KIRK DOUGLAS: My father.

BBC2

ANN DIAMOND: Toy theatres, what are they called?
GUEST: Toy theatres...

BBC

LORRAINE KELLY: Tell me a bit about yourself. What do you do?
INTERVIEWEE: Well, I'm a widow...
LORRAINE KELLY: Oh, great, that's great!

GMTV

1ST COMMENTATOR: I know geography, of course I know geography. Ask me a question on geography.
2ND COMMENTATOR: Who was the 3rd President of the United States?

SKY TV

DES O'CONNOR: You play indoor football?
CONTESTANT: Yes.
DES O'CONNOR: What is indoor football?
CONTESTANT: Football indoors.

ITV

PRESENTER: And who are you going to speak to when you finally learn Bulgarian?
CONTESTANT: Bulgarians!

CHANNEL 4

LORD SAINSBURY: My father opened a dairy in Drury Lane.
SUE LAWLEY: What did he sell?
LORD SAINSBURY: Well... dairy produce...

RADIO 4

RON (PHONE-IN CALLER): I'm now retired. I was a music teacher.

HENRY KELLY: What did you teach, Ron?

RON: Music, Henry.

CLASSIC FM

DAVID GLENCOURSE: We're now going over to talk to an eye-witness — tell me, what did you see?

EYEWITNESS: Nothing really — I ran down Regent Street.

DAVID GLENCOURSE: Well, what can you see now?

EYEWITNESS: Eros — I'm at Piccadilly Circus!

SKY NEWS

PATIENT: I get violent headaches.
DOCTOR: Where?
PATIENT: In my head.

"JIMMY'S, ITV

CONTESTANT: And I won a holiday in Turkey.
PAUL COYA: Where did you go?
CONTESTANT: Turkey.

BBC2

ROSS KING: So, tell me, do you have a girlfriend at school?
YOUNG BOY: No.
ROSS KING: Oh, come on, there must be someone you've got your eyes on!
YOUNG BOY: I go to a boys' school.

RADIO 5

WOMAN: When I told my mother, she didn't speak to me for two years.
KILROY SILK: Really? What did she say?
WOMAN: Nothing.

KILROY, ITV

CALLER: I would like to send birthday greetings to my wife, Dilys Williams.

KEITH OWEN: What's her name?

CALLER: Dilys Williams.

BBC WALES

Royalty

"I understand the man is Asian, but is there any other reason why he shot at the Prince of Wales?"

RICHARD LITTLEJOHN

REPORTER: Where did the fire start?

HRH DUKE OF YORK: It started in the Private Chapel.

REPORTER: What's that called?

HRH DUKE OF YORK: The Private Chapel.

ITN

"As a centurion, she should be shortly receiving a telegram from the Queen."

MIKE GIDDY

"When I say 'we' I mean it in the royal sense as there are quite a few of us here in the studio."

DAVE LEE TRAVIS

Rowing

"If Oxford had been in front the position would be reversed."

COMMENTATOR, BOAT RACE

Rugby

"Both players must stand behind each other..."

RAY FRENCH

"It takes two sides to make a Final, and Widnes have done just that."

RAY FRENCH

"Wigan edging farther and nearer to Wembley now..."

RAY FRENCH

"And he's got the icepack on his groin there, so possibly not the old shoulder injury..."

RAY FRENCH

"They [Wigan] are top of the league albeit only on a points difference."

MARTIN OPHIAH

"There's the Wigan players running to the dressing room. That's the sign of a side that wants to get on with the game."

RAY FRENCH

"England have had the great thoughts of theirs of winning the Triple Crown dashed from their hands."

BILL MCLAREN

"This is one bridge too far for Wigan to climb now."

GMR

Skating

"It's a two-man contest between Torvill and Dean and Gritschek and Platov."

RADIO 4

Snooker

"The thing about luck in snooker is that it's so fortuitous."

DAVID VINE

"And can you, perhaps, Ray, tell us what the mental side of Terry's thoughts will be at this time?"

TED LOWE

"Well, I suppose, psychologically speaking, someone's got to be one frame up at this stage in the game."

EDDIE CHARLTON

"I've played him a few times and he's a very tough
kettle of fish."

STEVE DAVIS

"If you're neutral, of course you're rooting for
James Wattana..."

LBC

"24 years old with shoulders so much older."

TED LOWE

"There's a very sad-looking Wattana, but you'd never know to look at his face."

TED LOWE

Tennis

"Relentlessly the barometer climbs on the weathervane of serving for Stich."

JOHN BARRETT

"Her best forehand is on her backhand side."

VIRGINIA WADE

"He [Courier] is basically playing goalie to Martin's Muhammed Ali."

CHRISTINE JANES

"She [Monica Seles] has so much control of the racket with those double-handed wrists."

VIRGINIA WADE

FRED PERRY: It's all a question of did he [Agassi] or didn't he practise?
COMMENTATOR: And I think the answer is did he?

RADIO 5

"...the return sent to the feet of the extended arm of Stich..."

JOHN BARRETT

"Edberg... he moves from side to side laterally."

JOHN BARRETT

"The referee, with one eye on the match and both eyes on the weather."

WIMBLEDON COMMENTATOR

"Martina's done extremely well here to put Jana in the extremely difficult position of having to serve for the match."

ANN JONES

Vociferously

"I do read vociferously."

GARY BUSHELL

"Margaret is nodding vociferously."

JENNI MURRAY

"James Small's back is being massaged vociferously."

BRETT PROCTOR

You can read

Colemanballs

every issue in

PRIVATE EYE

And if you enjoyed this book,
the best-selling first
Colemanballs
is still available, as are
Colemanballs 2, 3, 4, 5 and 6.